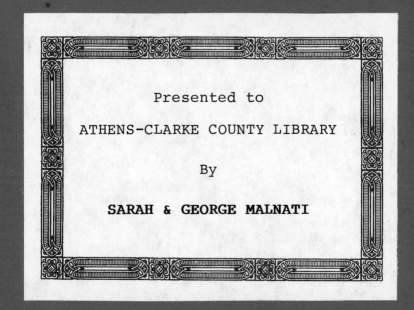

STUDY SKILLS FOR LIFE

STUDY SKILLS FOR LIFE

Based on the Works of

L. RON HUBBARD

Bridge

PUBLICATIONS, INC.

To the Parent or Teacher

Important information about the usage of this book is written on pages 129–131. Your familiarity with and application of the data in that section can help your son or daughter or your students get more out of this book.

Published by
Bridge Publications, Inc.
4751 Fountain Avenue
Los Angeles, California 90029

ISBN 0-88404-744-X

Contents

Introduction

Welcome to *Study Skills for Life*.

In this book you will learn HOW to learn anything you want. Whatever it is you want to learn, in school or out of school, you can learn IF you know how.

No one has ever taught you this before. You may remember your parents or teachers telling you to learn this, that or the other thing, but probably no one ever told you HOW to go about learning. And the truth is, no one knew it before.

Here's your chance.

Good luck!

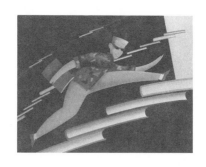

Chapter One:

Improving Your Ability to Learn

Improving Your Ability to Learn

It is a big world, but you can learn anything you want to about it. By "learning" we do not mean just getting facts crammed into your head. A fact is something that is known to be true. Getting more and more facts is not learning.

Learning is understanding new things and getting better ways to do things in life. Those who get along well in life never really stop studying and learning.

The good engineer keeps up with new ways. The skilled athlete continually reviews the progress of his sport. Any professional person keeps a stack of books near at hand and refers to them often.

But before you can learn about something you have to want to learn about that thing.

If you think you already know all there is to know about something, you will not be able to learn about it.

The first thing you have to decide is that you want to learn something.

Is there something you want to learn?

Once you have decided on something, the next step is to study it. What is study? Study is the act or process of learning something. It is a careful examination of something. The word originally meant "eagerness."

The only reason for studying something is to be able to apply what you have studied. There really isn't any other good reason for being educated. Many people think they study only so they can pass a test. That is not a very good reason for studying. If you studied something so you could **do** something in life, that would be a worthwhile reason for studying. If you wanted to learn how to repair tractors you would study this subject with the goal of being able to repair a tractor.

It has been discovered that there is a way to study anything so that when you have studied it, you can apply what you have learned. Like being able to dance or play basketball or sing or fix a car, being able to study is an ability.

In this book you are going to learn the keys to study. These are skills you will be able to use your whole life in anything you do. A person never really stops learning and once you know the information contained in this book you will have skills that will help you in anything you want to do.

So, do you want to learn how to learn?

Drill

Use a sheet of paper to write down your answers.

a. What is something you would really like to learn about?

b. How would it help you to learn about that?

c. What would you have to do to learn about that?

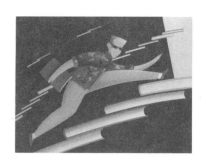

Chapter Two:

The Barriers to Study

The Barriers to Study

You may have had the experience of studying something and running into trouble. Maybe you even gave up trying to make sense of what you were studying.

If this has ever happened to you it means you ran into one of the barriers to study. Barriers are things that get in your way or stop your progress. There are three main barriers to being able to study any subject.

If you know and understand what these barriers are and what to do about them, your ability to study and learn can be greatly increased.

The First Barrier: Absence of Mass

The *mass* of a subject refers to the parts of that subject which are composed of matter and energy which exist in the real world. For example, if you were studying how to operate tractors, the *mass* would be an actual tractor. This is different than *words* about tractors or *ideas* about tractors or the *history* of tractors. The mass would be the tractor itself—the wheels, the motor, the seat, the steering wheel and all the other things that make up tractors.

If you are trying to learn a subject and you don't have the actual thing that you are studying about, it can be very difficult for you. Imagine trying to learn how to run a tractor without ever having seen a tractor!

If the mass of a subject is absent, you can actually feel squashed.

It can make you feel bent,

sort of spinny,

sort of dead,

or bored

or even angry.

If you are studying how to do something and you don't have the mass of it, this will be the result.

If you are studying about tractors, words on a page or someone telling you about tractors is no substitute for having an actual tractor there.

Photographs or motion pictures are helpful because they at least give the hope of the mass of a tractor.

It is important to understand that trying to learn about something when you don't have the mass of it available can produce the reactions shown earlier.

If you were trying to learn all about tractors but no one would show you any tractors or let you experience the mass of a tractor, you could wind up with a face that felt squashed, with headaches and with your stomach feeling funny. You might feel dizzy from time to time and often your eyes would hurt.

This knowledge is very useful. For example, if you were studying something and felt sick and it was traced back to a lack of mass, the way to fix this would be to supply the mass—the object itself or a reasonable substitute—and your sickness could rapidly clear up.

This barrier to study—the studying of something without its mass being around—produces some very definite reactions as we have seen above. Now that you know this, do the following drills.

Drill

Write down how you would handle these situations:

a. You just got a new stereo for your birthday. You are reading the manual that came with it but you start to feel sort of spinny and bent. The stereo is still in the box. What do you do?

b. Your friend is reading about motorcycles but has no idea what they look like. There are no motorcycles nearby to show him. What could you use instead?

Drill

Write down how you could get mass if you were studying about the ocean.

The Second Barrier: Too Steep a Gradient

A *gradient* is a slope upwards or downwards. A flight of stairs is an easy gradient up to the higher floors of a building. Trying to reach the upper floors by climbing up the outside wall of the building would be a steep gradient and impossible to do.

Learning something is best done with a gradual approach, step by step, level by level. When you learn on a gradient, you learn a little bit more and a little bit more. Finally, you can easily do things which would have been too complex or difficult in the beginning of your studies in an area.

The best approach to learning something is a gradient approach where you learn things step by step.

When a person hits too steep a gradient in studying a subject there is a confusion which results. The person can feel like he is reeling or swaying. This is the second barrier to study.

Say you were to find a person who was studying about engines and he was confused and sort of reeling.

You would know that there had been too much of a jump from studying one type of engine to studying a more complicated type of engine. The person did not really understand something about the first type of engine but jumped to studying the next type of engine and this was too steep a gradient for him.

The person assigns all of his difficulties to the new type of engine.

But the difficulty really lies at the tail end of his study of the first engine, the engine he felt he understood.

The remedy for too steep a gradient is to cut back the gradient. Find out when the person was not confused about what he was studying and then find out what new action he undertook to do. Find out what he felt he understood well just *before* he got all confused.

You will find that there is something in this area—the area where he felt he understood it—which he did not really understand.

When this is cleared up, the person will be able
to progress again.

This barrier of too steep a gradient is most easily seen when you are learning to *do* something. If you were just learning how to ride a motorcycle and someone demanded that you ride down a ramp and jump over a line of cars it would be very obvious that you had hit too steep a gradient.

When a person is found to be terribly confused on the second action he was supposed to do, it is a sure bet that he never really understood the *first* action.

Drill

Write down how you would handle this situation:

You are learning to dive. You have just learned to dive in the water from the side of the pool but you want to dive from the highest diving board ten feet off the water. What could you do to learn this at a proper gradient?

Drill

Write down a time you saw someone hit too steep a gradient. Describe what occurred. How could you have handled this using the data in this section of the book?

The Third—and Most Important—Barrier:
The Misunderstood Word

The third and most important barrier to study is the *misunderstood word*.

"Mis" means *not* or *wrongly*.

"Misunderstood" means *not understood* or *wrongly understood*.

A misunderstood word is a word which is *not understood* or a word which is *wrongly understood*.

It does not matter if the word is a big word:

alphabetical

or a little word:

him.

If you read past a word which you do not understand you can get some bad reactions. These are different from the reactions that can occur with the first two barriers to study.

Reading on past a word that was not understood . . .

can make you feel blank or washed out.

It can make you feel "not there"

and a sort of nervous upset feeling can follow after that.

The confusion or inability to understand or learn comes AFTER a word that you did not have defined and understood.

Later . . .

A misunderstood definition or an undefined word can cause a person to give up studying a subject entirely and leave a course or class. Leaving in this way is called a "blow."

A person does not necessarily "blow" because of the other barriers to study—lack of mass or too steep a gradient. These barriers simply produce physical reactions. But the misunderstood word can cause a student to blow.

The misunderstood word is much more important than the other two barriers to study. The misunderstood word is what determines a person's skill or talent in an area. People have been trying to test this for years but they did not know what it was.

It was simply the misunderstood word.

The misunderstood word is all that many study difficulties go back to. It is the misunderstood word that is the biggest factor involved with stupidity and many other things.

For example, if a person is not able to do things in the field of art, then there is some word that the person did not define or understand. This is followed by an inability to *do* things in the field of art.

This is very important because it tells you what can happen to a person's ability to do things in life. If he has misunderstood words, he may give up learning a subject or give up doing something. But it is more important to know that all you have to do to restore a person's ability to do something in life or to study something is to find the words he has misunderstood and get those words understood.

This is very simple technology.

The discovery of the misunderstood word actually opens the door to really becoming educated. And although this one has been given last, it is by far the most important of the barriers to study.

Drill

Write down how you would handle these situations:

a. You are reading a book. You get to the bottom of the page and realize that you don't remember any of what was written on the page. What should you do?

b. You do not feel like going back to class. Why might this be? How should you handle it?

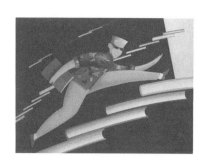

Chapter Three:

Handling
Misunderstood Words

Handling Misunderstood Words

When you come across a word you do not understand, it is important that you clear it up right away.

A misunderstood word will remain misunderstood until you "clear" the meaning of the word. "Clear" means to make understood. It means to learn the meaning of something. Once a word is fully understood, it is said to be "cleared."

Even a symbol can be misunderstood and must be cleared up. Imagine trying to work out the simple arithmetic problem $2 + 2 = ?$ if you did not know what 2, $+$, $=$ and $?$ meant.

There are certain steps you take in order to clear up a misunderstood word. This is an important skill and once you have learned it, it is something that will stay with you always and is a skill you will rely on for the rest of your life.

How to Clear a Word

1. Have a dictionary nearby while reading so that you can clear any misunderstood word or symbol you come across. A simple but good dictionary can be found that does not use hard-to-understand words in the definitions.

2. When you come across a word or symbol that you do not understand, the first thing to do is get a dictionary and look up the word. Look rapidly over the definitions to find which one fits the way the word is being used in what you are reading. Read that definition.

LEG 1. ————————

2. THE PART OF YOUR CLOTHES THAT COVERS A LEG. 3. ———————

LEG

DICTIONARY

Now make up sentences using the word in that way until you have a clear idea of that meaning of the word. You may have to make up ten or more sentences until you get a really clear idea of that meaning of the word. That is okay. The important thing is for you to really understand the meaning of the word.

THE INK SPILLED ALL OVER THE LEG OF HER PANTS.

HE TORE THE LEG ON THE FENCE.

SHE USED SOME RED CLOTH TO PATCH UP THE LEG OF HER PANTS.

3. Now clear each of the other definitions of that word, using each one in sentences until you clearly understand each definition.

When a word has several different definitions, you cannot limit your understanding of the word to one definition only and call the word "understood." You must be able to understand the word later when you read it again and it is being used in a different way.

When you are clearing up a word you do not have to clear the technical or specialized definitions such as a specialized mathematics definition for the word or a technical definition from a branch of science, etc.

Sometimes a dictionary gives definitions of a word that are no longer used. These are called "obsolete" definitions and you do not have to clear those.

Also, some dictionaries give definitions of words that were used in ancient times and which are no longer used by people. These are called "archaic" definitions and you do not have to clear those.

The only time you would have to clear a specialized or technical or obsolete or archaic definition is when it is being used that way in what you were reading when you came across it.

4. The next thing to do is to clear the derivation of the word. The derivation is the explanation of where the word came from originally. This will help you to get a basic understanding of the word.

5. Sometimes words are used in ways that cannot be understood simply from the ordinary meanings of the words. For example, you might read the phrase "all in" in the sentence "Joe did not want to go to the party because he was feeling all in." You cannot figure out what is meant by the phrase "all in" simply by looking up "all" and "in." You have to look up the phrase itself and in this case it would be found under the word "all" in the dictionary and it means "very tired." When words are used this way, it is called an "idiom." There are many idioms in the language. When you say to a friend, "Joe is up to his neck in trouble" you mean that Joe is in a lot of trouble. It does not actually have anything to do with his neck.

If the word you are clearing has idioms, you do clear these as well.

6. If there is any other information given about the word such as a note on the usage of the word, be sure to read and understand this.

If words are listed which mean nearly the same thing as the word you are clearing be sure to read and understand these as well. These are called "synonyms." For instance, after the definition of the word "large" the dictionary might list "big," "huge," "great" and "tremendous" as synonyms.

All this other information will help to give you a full understanding of the word.

7. While clearing a word, if you find a misunderstood word or symbol in the definition, you should clear it right away using the procedure in steps 1–6 above. When this is done, return to the definition you were clearing. (The symbols and abbreviations used in the dictionary are usually given in the front of the dictionary.)

If you find yourself spending a lot of time clearing words within definitions of words, you should get a simpler dictionary. A good dictionary will enable you to clear a word without having to look up a lot of other words while doing that.

Anytime you are reading or studying and the material becomes hard to grasp, or you can't seem to understand what you are reading or you feel blank, washed out or feel like throwing the book down, *realize that you have gone past a misunderstood word*. Don't go any further, but go back to just *before* you got into difficulty, find the misunderstood word and clear it.

Once you have looked up the word and fully understood it, then restudy the book from that point. It should now be easy to understand. If it isn't, there is another word that you don't understand. You must find it and get it looked up and fully understood.

Knowing the steps of how to clear a word is one of the most important parts of learning. Once you know how to clear a word there is no word you cannot understand.

Drill

Practice the steps of clearing up a word until you know the steps of doing this and can do them easily. Do this with the words "home," "shoe" and "chimney."

Drill

Remember a word or find a word you know you do not understand or are unsure of and clear it using a dictionary.

Drill

Go back through the section "Handling Misunderstood Words" and look for any words you do not fully understand. Clear these in the dictionary and restudy the section as you go. Write down what words you found and cleared.

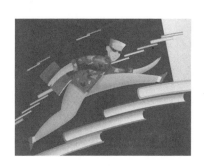

Chapter Four:

The Use of Demonstration

Demonstration and Learning

The word *demonstration* means "the act or process of showing something or of showing how something operates or works." It comes from the Latin word *demonstrare*, which means "to point out, show, prove."

Demonstrating things has a lot of use in learning. It shows whether or not someone really understands what he is studying or if he can apply what he has learned.

In studying, a student can do a "demonstration" or "demo" with something called a "demo kit." A demo kit consists of various small objects such as corks, caps, paper clips, pen tops, rubber bands, etc. The student uses his hands and the pieces of his demo kit to demonstrate an idea or principle.

If a student ran into something he couldn't quite figure out, a demo kit would assist him to understand it. By making the different pieces of the demo kit represent the objects he is studying about, the student can move them around and see more clearly how they relate to each other, etc.

By doing demonstrations of what he is studying, the student is getting mass to go along with the ideas studied.

OKAY, THIS IS SUE, AND SHE GOES OVER TO THE CORNER AND . . .

Drill

Using your demo kit, demonstrate the following things about the barriers to study which you have learned about earlier in this book:

a. How you would recognize that you had lack of mass and how you would handle this.

b. How you would recognize that you were at too steep a gradient and how you would handle this.

c. How you would know you have a misunderstood word and how you would handle this.

Clay Demonstrations

Another form of demonstration is using clay figures to demonstrate a concept or principle. These are called clay demonstrations or clay demos. Clay demos can help you understand better what you are studying. Doing clay demos accomplishes several things:

1. They make the materials being studied real to the student by making him DEMONSTRATE them in clay.

2. They give a proper balance of mass and significance.

3. Clay demos teach the student to apply.

If you come across something you cannot figure out, you can work it out in clay.

How to Do a Clay Demo

In doing a clay demo, the clay gives mass. Then a label is added to each piece of clay in the demonstration that says what the thing is.

Say you wanted to do a clay demo of a pencil. First, make a thin roll of clay. This is the pencil lead.

You would make a label using a strip of paper and write on it with a pen "LEAD" and stick it on the thin roll of clay.

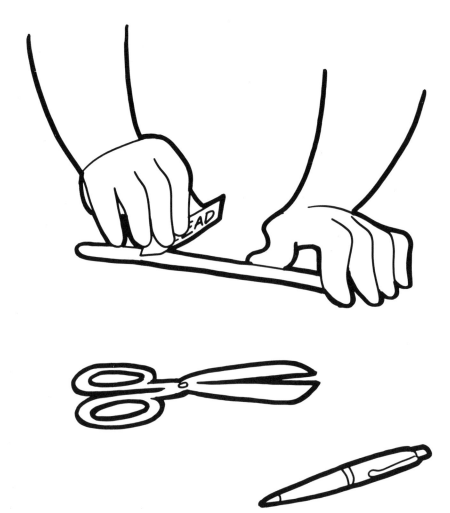

Next, put on another layer of clay with the thin roll sticking out a little bit at one end. This is the wood part of the pencil, so you would make a label that said "WOOD" and stick it on.

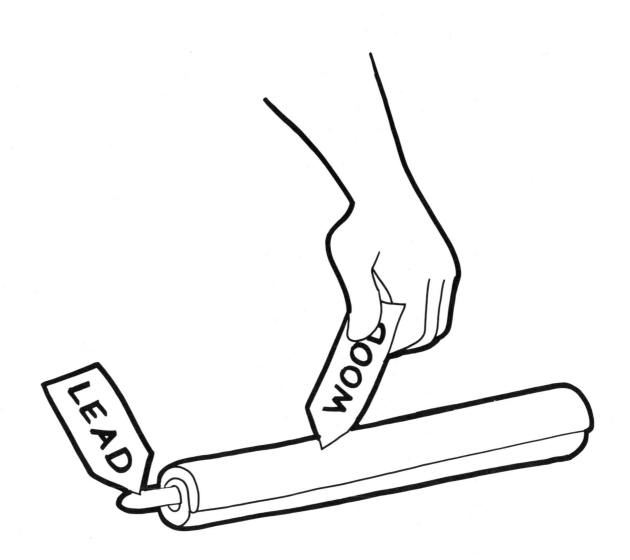

Then you put another little piece of clay on the end. This is the rubber eraser so you would write "RUBBER" on a label and stick it on that piece of clay.

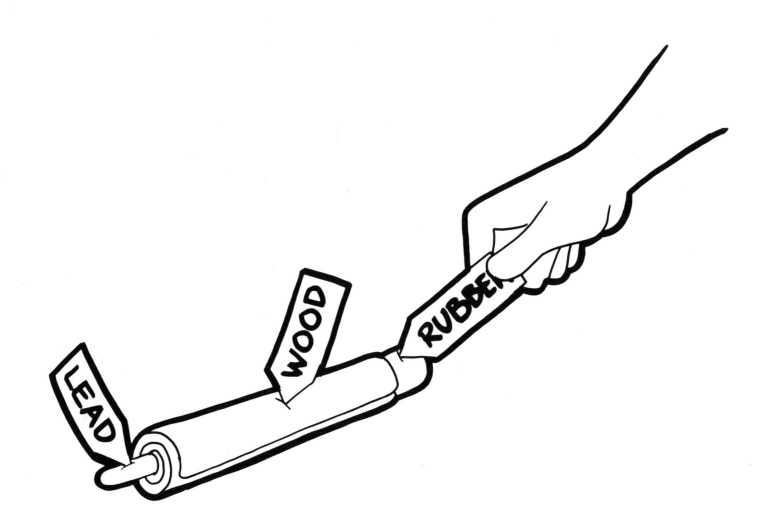

Finally, you make a label for the whole thing, "PENCIL."

You could show someone you understand something by removing the overall label and then getting another person to examine your clay demo. He would just look and figure out what you had demonstrated. If he could tell what you were demonstrating just from the clay and without asking you any questions and with you not saying anything, that would show that you understood what you had studied well enough to demonstrate it in clay to another person.

Clay Demo Size

Clay demos must be large.

One of the purposes of clay demonstrations is to make the materials being studied real to a person. If your clay demo is small (less mass), it may not provide enough mass for you. And long experience has shown that BIG clay demos are more successful in helping to increase understanding.

Making the parts of a clay demo artistic is not important. The forms can be crude.

Labeling Clay Demonstrations

Each separate thing is labeled that is part of a clay demonstration, no matter how crude the label is. Students usually do labels with scraps of paper written on with a ballpoint. When cutting out a label, a point is put on one end, making it easy to stick the label into the clay.

Each time you make an object you label it. You make the first object of your clay demo, label it, make the second object, label it, make the third object, label it and so on.

Anything can be demonstrated in clay. You can even show a thought. Use a thin ring of clay to show a thought or idea. Here is a clay demo of a person thinking about a ball.

If you don't understand something in life or in what you are studying, you can work it out in clay and understand it better. Clay demos are an important part of good study skills.

Drill

Use a sheet of paper to write down your answer.

How could you use clay demos to help you understand something better? Give an example of something specific.

Sketching

Sketching is also part of demonstration and part of working things out.

Someone sitting at his desk trying to work something out may not have any clay to hand to work it out with, but he could work it out with a paper and pencil, and draw a picture of it or a graph of it. This would help him understand it better.

An obvious example is a ship's navigator who, instead of trying to work it all out in his head with some foggy concept of where he is simply graphs the sailing plan and progress on a chart.

Drill

Use sketching to do a demonstration of a student clearing a misunderstood word.

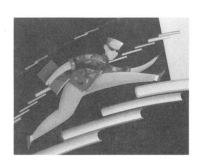

Chapter Five:

Checkouts

Checkouts

A checkout is the action of examining a student's knowledge of the material he is studying. This is an excellent way of seeing whether someone understands what he has studied.

If you give someone a checkout on something he has studied you will be able to see if he really understands what he's studied.

It will never do a student any good in life to *know* some facts. The student is expected to *use* facts.

Therefore, it is important to remember that all checkouts must test the student's understanding of what he has studied.

A proper checkout is not a test of whether someone can memorize what he has read and repeat it back. That is no proof that he understands and can apply what he has studied.

Example of a Checkout

Say you want to check out a friend on the manual which tells him how to operate his new motorcycle.

Go over the first part of the material you are checking him out on and pick out a few uncommon words. Ask the student to define each and demonstrate its use in a made-up sentence. If he couldn't define the words or use them in sentences you would know he does not understand his materials well. He would "flunk" the checkout and would have to look up the words he did not understand and restudy his materials.

You would have to make sure that you also know what the words mean before you start to check him out.

When your friend shows he understands the words, you ask him questions about the materials that get him to show he understands how the materials are applied. Questions like, "Now this rule here about always wearing a helmet while riding, how come there'd be such a rule?" If the student couldn't imagine why, you would send him back to the words just before that rule to find the one he hadn't grasped.

In a checkout, the person must show that he understands the words and understands how the materials are applied.

Giving Checkouts

A correct checkout is done only by making the person being tested answer:

a. The meanings of the words (redefining the words used in his own words and demonstrating their use in his own made-up sentences), and

b. Demonstrating how the data is used.

Checkouts must include demonstrations of the materials using a demo kit. In a checkout, you should ask questions that require an ability to *apply* the material. Give the person you are checking out a situation and have him tell you how he would handle it.

Before any person may give another a checkout, he must himself have read the material. If he is checking out someone on a taped lecture, he must have listened to the lecture. This will make it possible to give a good checkout.

This is not a checkout!

This is an example of a correct checkout.

When the checkout of the words is completed, a checkout is done on the materials.

Here's what to do if you flunk a checkout:

124

Being able to do a good checkout is an important study skill. You can tell if a person really understands something by giving him a checkout on it.

Drill

a. Find another student or a friend to do this drill with. Get a copy of something that both of you have studied and are familiar with. (If there are no materials which you have both studied, then choose something for use in the drill and both of you study it.) Ask the person irrelevant questions about this material and demand that he quote certain sentences and phrases from it word for word. Write down what you did and what occurred.

b. Now give the other person a standard checkout on the above materials, using the data in the above chapter. Write down what you did and what occurred.

CONGRATULATIONS!

You have completed *Study Skills for Life*.

The skills you have learned, if you use them, can help you greatly in anything you want to do in life. A person never really stops learning and knowing how to study is something you can use every day. It is very well done that you have accomplished this.

The real benefit of your new study skills comes when you apply them. Whatever you want to learn in life, you can learn it faster and better by using what you learned in this book.

Important Information for Parents and Teachers

This book has been published to fill an important need.

We live now in an instruction-book world. Our civilization is highly technical.

Formal education today goes into one's twenties, nearly a third of a lifetime. But what happens when a person leaves school? Can he *do* what he studied? And factually, education begins *before* a person learns to speak and continues throughout his entire life. Can he *do* what he has studied outside of the classrooms of his school days?

Any young person's future success and happiness are dependent on his ability to learn. Innately, this ability is very strong. Young children, for instance, possess an almost boundless fascination about everything in life. A curiosity and eagerness to explore and learn is turned on "high" at a very young age.

Young people are confronted with so many things they don't yet understand. They have been told that learning is the key to their future. But it is a mean trick to tell someone that he must learn and then not teach him the skills he needs to enable him to learn.

Study Skills for Life contains fundamental principles of L. Ron Hubbard's researches into the field of education, where he isolated the basics which underlie all forms of learning. His breakthroughs resulted in Study Technology, the first subject which actually deals with HOW to learn. Study Technology is basic to any specific subject since it deals with learning itself, the barriers to learning and remedies for these barriers.

Study Skills for Life presents the fundamentals of Study Technology at a level that a young person can assimilate, understand and *use*. It is a breakthrough in the field of learning and education for preteenagers and teenagers.

Using the Book for Maximum Benefit

Reading Level

The book is written so that a person can study it by himself. It has been written for young people ages twelve through fifteen, though people younger than twelve have successfully used the book.

Drills

There are drills throughout the book which get the reader to *apply* what he has read. These are key to gaining the most from the book and the student should be encouraged to do them thoroughly.

Familiarity

In working with a son or daughter on the book or in using it in a classroom, it will help if you have read the book first and are familiar with its contents. Though simply written, the data presented here are not to be found in any previously published book on education or learning. The concepts are totally original with the researches of L. Ron Hubbard into the field of education and his discoveries on the mental phenomena which block learning, the physiological manifestations which result from these blocks and the specific remedies for each one.

Ensuring Understanding

In giving this book to your son or daughter and in working with him or her on the book or in using it in a classroom situation, there is one very important datum about study of which you should be aware:

THE ONLY REASON A PERSON GIVES UP A STUDY OR BECOMES CONFUSED OR UNABLE TO LEARN IS BECAUSE HE HAS GONE PAST A WORD THAT WAS NOT UNDERSTOOD.

The confusion or inability to grasp or learn comes AFTER a word that the person did not have defined and understood.

Have you ever had the experience of coming to the end of a page and realizing you didn't know what you had read? Well, somewhere earlier on that page you went past a word that you had no definition for or an incorrect definition for.

Here's an example. "It was found that when the crepuscule arrived the children were quieter and when it was not present, they were livelier." You see what happens. You think you don't understand the whole idea, but the inability to understand came entirely from the one word you could not define, *crepuscule*, which means twilight or darkness.

The datum about not going past an undefined word is the most important datum in study and is thoroughly covered in the book on pages 42–60. Every subject a person has taken up and then abandoned or done poorly at had its words which the person failed to get defined. It is the most important barrier to study and a parent or teacher should be familiar with this datum. The phenomena which occur after a person has unknowingly encountered a word he or she did not understand are quite distinct and easily recognized once you know what you are looking at.

As simple as it seems, many of the tribulations in students' lives can be traced back to words they have not understood in their study materials or in life.

Use as a Reference Book

After someone has read the book and learned these study skills, he can and should be referred back to his materials whenever necessary during his future studies. As startling as it may seem, a workable technology of how to study something was foreign to the field of education before L. Ron Hubbard's researches in the area. *Study Skills for Life* can be used time and time again as a reminder of the basics of successful learning.

Further Information

Numerous schools across the United States and throughout Europe now utilize Mr. Hubbard's study technology to promote faster learning with increased comprehension.

If you or your child or student encounter any difficulties in reading or applying the data in this book there are addresses of schools and institutions on the following pages you can contact. These organizations make exclusive use of study technology and will be happy to provide any assistance needed as well as provide further information about these new advances in education.

There is also a toll-free number you can call for assistance or for further information: (1-800-424-5397).

When a person knows how to gain more knowledge, his enthusiasm for learning will never become stale. Once a person grasps the tools contained here these will become a natural part of his approach to living and he will use them throughout all his activities in life.

The fundamentals contained in *Study Skills for Life* are sweeping discoveries in the field of education and they open the gates to learning and application.

When a person has learned how to learn, all knowledge becomes available to him, assuring that, whatever his fields of interest, he will have the greatest possible chance for fulfillment and success.

About the Author

L. Ron Hubbard was no stranger to education. Although his main profession was that of a professional writer, in a long, event-filled and productive life he spent thousands of hours researching in the education field, lecturing and teaching.

He was born in Tilden, Nebraska on 13 March 1911, and his early years were spent on his grandfather's ranch in the wilds of Montana. As the son of a US Navy commander, he was well on the way to becoming a seasoned traveler by the age of eight, and by the time he was nineteen he had logged over a quarter of a million miles.

He enrolled in George Washington University in 1930, taking classes in mathematics and engineering. But his was not a quiet academic life. He took up flying in the pioneer days of aviation, learning to pilot first glider planes and then powered aircraft. He worked as a freelance reporter and photographer. He directed expeditions to the Caribbean and Puerto Rico, and later, to Alaska. The world was his classroom and he studied voraciously, gathering experience which provided the background for his later writings, research and discoveries.

Some of his first published articles were nonfiction, based upon his aviation experience. Soon he began to draw from his travels to produce a wide variety of fiction stories and novels: adventure, mystery, westerns, fantasy and science fiction.

The proceeds from his fiction writing funded his main line of research and exploration—how to improve the human condition. His nonfiction works cover such diverse subjects as drug rehabilitation, marriage and family, success at work, statistical analysis, public relations, art, marketing and much, much more. But he did more than write books—he also delivered over 6,000 lectures and conducted courses to impart his own discoveries to others.

However, in order to learn, one must be able to read and understand. Therefore, L. Ron Hubbard tackled the problem of teaching others how to study. His research uncovered the basic reason for the failure of a student to grasp any subject. He discovered the barriers to full comprehension of what one is studying, and developed methods by which anyone can improve his ability to learn and to *apply* the data that he is being taught. He wrote a considerable body of work on this subject, which he termed *study technology*.

L. Ron Hubbard's advanced technology of study is now used by an estimated two million students and thousands of teachers in universities and school systems internationally. His educational materials have been translated into twelve languages to meet this worldwide demand for the first truly *workable* technology of how to study. Organizations delivering L. Ron Hubbard's study technology have been established in the United States, Australia, South Africa, Canada, Austria, Great Britain, Pakistan, Mexico, Germany, Denmark, France, Italy, Venezuela and China.

L. Ron Hubbard departed his body on 24 January 1986. His contributions to the world of education have meant new hope, better understanding and increased ability for millions of students and educators the world over.

Additional Books for Students by L. Ron Hubbard

Learning How to Learn • For children, knowing how to read and being able to understand and *apply* what they read is the real key to success in their lives. With the simple steps taught in this book, written for young students, learning can become an exciting and rewarding experience.

How to Use a Dictionary Picture Book for Children • One of the ingredients of a quality education is giving a student the tools he needs to study successfully on his own. No matter the subject or field being learned, one has to know how to use the dictionary to clearly understand the meaning of words. This book contains the secret of how to put education into action.

Grammar and Communication • The ability to communicate is vital to happiness and self-confidence. But getting one's communication across is dependent upon being able to speak and write correctly. The unique approach to grammar taught in this book can open the world of words to a child—granting him the strong sense of self-esteem which results from the ability to read well, write clearly and communicate effectively.

When the young can learn and think for themselves, the world is an open book.

TO ORDER THESE BOOKS OR TO GET MORE INFORMATION ON L. RON HUBBARD'S STUDY TECHNOLOGY, CALL: 1-800-424-5397

For more information on educational books and materials by L. Ron Hubbard, contact your nearest distributor:

Association for Better Living
and Education International
6331 Hollywood Blvd., Suite 700
Hollywood, California 90028

Association for Better Living
and Education Canada
696 Yonge Street
Toronto, Ontario,
Canada M4Y 2A7

Association for Better Living
and Education East US
349 W. 48th Street
New York, NY 10036

Association for Better Living
and Education Europe
Sankt Nikolaj Vej 4-6
1953 Frederiksberg
Copenhagen, Denmark

Instituto de Tecnologia para la
Educacion A.C.
Tetla #6
Colonia Ruiz Cortines
Delegación Coyoacán
64630 México D.F.

Association for Better Living
and Education United Kingdom
Saint Hill Manor
East Grinstead, W. Sussex
England RH19 4JY

Association for Better Living
and Education Australia and
New Zealand
201 Castlereagh St.
Sydney NSW 2000, Australia

Association for Better Living
and Education Africa
2nd Floor, Security Building
95 Commissioner St.
Johannesburg 2001, South Africa

Association for Better Living
and Education Italy
via Nerino, 8
20123 Milano, Italy

You can also contact any of the groups and organizations on the following pages which use L. Ron Hubbard's study technology.

Applied Scholastics Groups and Organizations

Applied Scholastics International
7060 Hollywood Blvd., Suite 200
Los Angeles, California 90028

United States of America

Arizona

Phoenix Renaissance Academy, Inc.
4330 N. 62nd St., #128
Phoenix, Arizona 85251

California

Ability Academy
PO Box 601091
San Diego, California 92160

Ability Plus School—La Canada
4490 Cornishon Ave.
La Canada, California 91011

Ability Plus School—Orange
County
333 S. Prospect
Orange, California 92669

Ability Plus School—Woodland
Hills
22626 Burton Street
West Hills, California 91304

Academy for Smart Kids
4632 Russell Ave.
Los Angeles, California 90027

Applied Scholastics—Crescenta
Valley
7944 Day Street
Sunland, California 91040

Applied Scholastics—Los Angeles
503 Central Ave.
Glendale, California 91203

Applied Scholastics—San Francisco
39355 California St. #107
Fremont, California 94538

Delphi Academy—Los Angeles
4490 Cornishon Ave.
La Canada, California 91011

Delphi Academy—Sacramento
5325 Engle Rd. #600
Carmichael, California 95608

Delphi Academy—San Francisco
445 E. Charleston Rd. #7
Palo Alto, California 94306

Expansion Consultants, Inc.
1053 Rosedale Ave.
Glendale, California 91201

Gavilan Hills School
17305 Santa Rosa Mine Road
Gavilan Hills, California 92370

Golden Gate Apple School
379 Colusa Ave.
Kensington, California 94707

Jane Warner's School
2704 N. Fair Oaks Ave.
Altadena, California 91001

Karen Aranas Tutoring Center
933 Edward Ave. #24
Santa Rosa, California 95401

Kids' World School
1220 N. Berendo Ave.
Los Angeles, California 90029

The Learning Bridge
593 4th Ave.
San Francisco, California 94118

The Learning Connection
2528 Canyon Drive
Hollywood, California 90068

The Learning Solution
4274 Caledonia Way
Los Angeles, California 90065

Lewis Carroll Academy of the Arts
5425 Cahuenga Blvd.
N. Hollywood, California 91601

Los Gatos Academy
14969 Los Gatos Almaden Rd.
Los Gatos, California 95032

Mojave Desert School
44579 Temescal
Newberry Springs, California 92365

Pinewood Academy
4490 Cornishon Ave.
La Canada, California 91011

Punkin School
1839 N. Kenmore Ave.
Los Angeles, California 90027

Real School
50 El Camino
Corte Madera, California 94925

Smart Apple Tutoring Service
1310 Chuckwagon Dr.
Sacramento, California 95834

VenturePlan
3300 Foothill Blvd.
Box 12570
La Crescenta, California 91224

Colorado

Applied Scholastics—Colorado
3 Paonia
Littleton, Colorado 80127

Rocky Mountain Academy
781 S. Federal
Denver, Colorado 80219

Connecticut

Ability Plus Connecticut
256 Brainard Hill Road
Higganum, Connecticut 06441

Florida

A Country Place
Rt. 1 350 L
Bushnell, Florida 33513

Applied Scholastics—Miami
2557 SW 31st Ave.
Miami, Florida 33133

A To Be School, Inc.
520 Cleveland Street
Clearwater, Florida 34615

Jefferson Academy, Inc.
1301 N. Highland Ave.
Clearwater, Florida 34615

Studema International
100 Pierce, Suite 602
Clearwater, Florida 34617

The Parents' Cooperative School
1600 E. Robinson #100
Orlando, Florida 32803

TRUE School, Inc.
1831 Drew Street
Clearwater, Florida 34625

Georgia

Lafayette Academy
2417 Canton Road
Marietta, Georgia 30066

Illinois

The Learning School, Inc.
864 E. Northwest Hwy.
Mount Prospect, Illinois 60056

Massachusetts

Applied Scholastics—New England
1500 Main Street, Suite 4
Weymouth, Massachusetts 02190

Delphi Academy—Boston
564 Blue Hill Ave.
Milton, Massachusetts 02186

Michigan

Cedars Center
1602 W. 3rd Ave.
Flint, Michigan 48504

Recording Institute of Detroit, Inc.
14611 E. Nine Mile Road
East Detroit, Michigan 48021

Missouri

Ability School—St. Louis
14298 Olive St. Road
St. Louis, Missouri 63017

New Hampshire

Bear Hill School, Inc.
PO Box 417
Pittsfield, New Hampshire 03263

New Jersey

Ability School—New Jersey
192 W. Demarest Ave.
Englewood, New Jersey 07631

The Freedom School
U8 Kingswick Apts.
Thorofare, New Jersey 08086

Ohio

Applied Scholastics—Ohio
101 W. Dunedin Rd.
Columbus, Ohio 43214

Oregon

Columbia Academy, Inc.
1808 SE Belmont
Portland, Oregon 97214

The Delphian School—Oregon
20950 SW Rock Creek Road
Sheridan, Oregon 97378

Eagle Oak School
PO Box 12
Bridal Veil, Oregon 97010

Texas

Austin Academy of Higher
Learning
12002 N. Lamar
Austin, Texas 78753

Perfect Schooling, Inc.
402 Town and Country Village
Houston, Texas 77024

Utah

Ability School—Utah
913 E. Syrena Circle
Sandy, Utah 89094

Virginia

Chesapeake Ability School
5533 Industrial Dr.
Springfield, Virginia 22151

Washington

Keller Learning Center
1141 NW Market Street
Seattle, Washington 98107

Wyoming

Great American Ski School
PO Box 427
Jackson, Wyoming 83001

Canada

Applied Scholastics (National
Office)
840 Pape Ave., Suite 209
Toronto, Ontario M4K 3T6
Canada

Education Alive—Halifax
2130 Armcrescent West
Halifax, Nova Scotia B3L 3E3
Canada

Education Alive—Kentville
27 James Street
Kentville, Nova Scotia B4N 2A1
Canada

Education Alive—Toronto
840 Pape Ave., Suite 201
Toronto, Ontario M4K 3T6
Canada

Effective Education School
8920 Charles Street
Richmond, British Columbia
V6X 1G1
Canada

Progressive Academy
12245 131st Street
Edmonton, Alberta T5L 1M8
Canada

Simon Berube Educational Services
114 Bourassa
St. Luc, Québec J0J 2A0
Canada

Toronto Ability School
85 41st Street
Toronto, Ontario M8W 3P1
Canada

Wise Owl Tutoring
342 Blackthorn Ave.
Toronto, Ontario M6N 3J3
Canada

United Kingdom

Effective Education Association
East Grinstead
31A High Street
East Grinstead, W. Sussex
RH19 3AF
England

Effective Education Association
London
2C Falkland Rd. Kentish Town
London NW5
England

Effective Education Association
Scotland
31 St. Katharine's Brae
Liberton, Edinburgh EH16 6PY
Scotland

Effective Education Association
Sunderland
9 Catherine Tce.
Newkyo, Stanley, Co. Durham
DH9 7TP
England

Greenfields School
Priory Road—Forest Row
E. Sussex RH18 53D
England

Austria

Kreativ College
Rienosslgasse 12
1040 Wien, Austria

Belgium

Brussels Ability School
Rue Auguste Lambiotte 23
1030 Bruxelles
Belgium

Scandinavian Ability School
Ave. des Orchidees 38
1410 Waterloo
Belgium

Denmark

Amager International School
5th Floor, Graekenlandsvej 51-53
2300 Copenhagen S, Denmark

Applied Scholastics (European
Office)
F. F. Ulriksgade 13
2100 Copenhagen O, Denmark

Applied Scholastics—Denmark
F. F. Ulriksgade 13
2100 Copenhagen O, Denmark

Foreningen for Effektiv
Grunduddannelse Aarhus
Hammervaenget 22
8310 Tranbjerg, Denmark

Foreningen for Effektiv
Grunduddannelse Amager
Graekenlandsvej 53
2300 Copenhagen S, Denmark

Foreningen for Effektiv
Grunduddannelse Birkerod
Kongevejen 110 B
3460 Birkerod, Denmark

Foreningen for Effektiv
Grunduddannelse Brondby
Strand
Hyttebovej 20
2660 Brondby Strand, Denmark

Foreningen for Effektiv
Grunduddannelse Bronshoj
Klintevej 40
2700 Bronshoj, Denmark

Foreningen for Effektiv
Grunduddannelse Dania
Daniavej 60 Assens
9550 Mariager, Denmark

Foreningen for Effektiv
Grunduddannelse Dania
Erhvervscenter
Daniavej 60 Assens
9550 Mariager, Denmark

Foreningen for Effektiv
Grunduddannelse Glostrup
Falkevej 20
2600 Glostrup, Denmark

Foreningen for Effektiv
Grunduddannelse Grinsted
Gronlandsvej 2
7290 Grinsted, Denmark

Foreningen for Effektiv
Grunduddannelse Hvidovre
Hvidovre Alle 17
2650 Hvidovre, Denmark

Foreningen for Effektiv
Grunduddannelse Kalundborg
Dalsvinget 5
4400 Kalundborg, Denmark

Foreningen for Effektiv
Grunduddannelse Koge
Straedet 6
Stroby Egede
4600 Koge, Denmark

Foreningen for Effektiv
Grunduddannelse Naestved
H. C. Lumbyesvej 102
4700 Naestved, Denmark

Foreningen for Effektiv
Grunduddannelse Norrebro
Ravnsborggade 6, 5
2200 Copenhagen N, Denmark

Foreningen for Effektiv
Grunduddannelse Norre Sundby
Jorgenbertelsvej 17 A, 1tv
9400 Norre Sundby, Denmark

Foreningen for Effektiv
Grunduddannelse Olstykke
Sajisnej 21
3650 Olstykke, Denmark

Foreningen for Effektiv
Grunduddannelse Osterbro
F. F. Ulriksgade 13
2100 Copenhagen O, Denmark

Foreningen for Effektiv
Grunduddannelse Risskov
Flintebakken 60
8240 Risskov, Denmark

Foreningen for Effektiv
Grunduddannelse Silkeborg
Chr. D. 8. vej 12.1
8600 Silkeborg, Denmark

Foreningen for Effektiv
Grunduddannelse Slagelse
Sct. Mikkelsgade 23
4200 Slagelse, Denmark

Foreningen for Effektiv
Grunduddannelse Tastrup
Kogevej 11
2630 Tastrup, Denmark

Foreningen for Effektiv
Grunduddannelse Vadum
Ulrik Burihovej 69
9330 Vadum, Denmark

Foreningen for Effektiv
Grunduddannelse Vojens
Vestergade 58
6100 Haderslev, Denmark

Kildeskolen
Roskildevej 158
2500 Valby, Denmark

France

Aptitudes
11 rue Palluat de Besset
42000 St. Etienne, France

Ecole de l'éveil
11 passage Courtois
75011 Paris, France

Education France
16 rue du Bac
75007 Paris, France

Institute d'Aide a l'Etude
12 impasse Bonnave
42000 St. Etienne, France

Irene Chartry Tutoring Service
27 rue Andre Cayron
92600 Asnieres, France

Joel Payan Tutoring Services
43 rue Pierre Brossolette
92600 Asnieres, France

La Méthode pour apprendre
88 rue de la Rivière
72000 Le Mans, France

Le Cours pour apprendre
16 rue du Bac
75007 Paris, France

Management Distribution
43 rue Volney
49000 Angers, France

Germany

Applied Scholastics—Deutschland
Unter Buschweg 118
5000 Köln, Germany

Institut Siebrecht
Unter Buschweg 118
5000 Köln, Germany

Institut Thonke
Am Neuhanskothen 51
5620 Velbert 11
Germany

Italy

Associazione Studio Moderno
Piazza Cittadella, 13
41100 Modena, Italy

Holland

Stichting voor Effectief Onderwijs
Goudsbloemstraat 205
1015 JN Amsterdam, Holland

Sweden

Applied Scholastics—Sweden
Terrangvegen 39
S-126 61 Hagersten, Sweden

Daghemmet U-Care
Grusasgrand 88
S-122 49 Enskede, Sweden

Fritidshemmet Robin Hood
Terrangvegen 39
S-126 61 Hagersten, Sweden

Maasen Daghem
Nedre Bergsvagen 4
S-126 34 Hagersten, Sweden

Studema-Skolan
Terrangvegen 39
S-126 61
Hagersten, Sweden

Switzerland

Verein ZIEL
Postfach 5114
CH-6002 Luzern, Switzerland

Australia

Ability Plus
32 Ryan St.
Northcote Victoria 3070
Australia

Applied Scholastics—Canberra
36 Ebden St.
GPO Box 1910
Ainslie, Canberra, ACT 2602
Australia

Applied Scholastics—Sydney
Suite 3, Level 3
647 George St.
Sydney NSW 2000
Australia

Applied Scholastics Training Centre
#404, 3 Smail St.
Broadway NSW 2007
Australia

Athena School
697 Princes Highway
Tempe NSW 2044
Australia

I Can Enhancements
1/23 Glebe Point Rd.
Glebe NSW 2037
Australia

Jennie Gellie Tutoring Services
21 Railway Parade
Hazelbrook NSW 2779
Australia

Yarralinda School
319 Canterbury Road
Ringwood, Victoria 3134
Australia

Malaysia

Applied Scholastics Institute
No. 42-2A, Jalan Tun Sambanthan
50470 Kuala Lumpur
Malaysia

Pakistan

Effective Education Association—
  Karachi
348 CP Berar Society, Block 7/8
Dhoraji Colony
Karachi-5, Pakistan

Africa

A+ School
28 Church Street
Halfway House
Pretoria 1685, South Africa

Education Alive—Cape Town
51 Station Road
Observatory
Cape Town 7925, South Africa

Education Alive—Johannesburg
3rd Floor CDH House
217 Jeppe Street
Johannesburg 2001, South Africa

Education Alive (National Office)
3rd Floor CDH House
217 Jeppe Street
Johannesburg 2001, South Africa

Education Alive School
3rd Floor CDH House
217 Jeppe Street
Johannesburg 2001, South Africa

Latin America

Colombia

Ayuda Escolar
Cra 28 No. 91-39
Sante Fe de Bogota
Colombia

México

Educacion Del Mañana
Cordobanes 47
Col. San Jose Insurgentes
03900 México D.F.

Grupo Iniciativa
Calzada de Tlalpan #934
Col. Nativitas
03500 México D.F.

ITE de Guadalajara
Jazmin 376 S.R.
Guadalajara, Jalisco
México

ITE de Jalapa
Corregidora #24-A
Col. Centro
Jalapa, Veracruz
México

Venezuela

Educacion Viva
Apartado Postal 63265 Chacaito
Caracas, Venezuela

Inventec
c/o Instituto Tecnico Aristotele
Av. La Salle, Urb Los Caobos
Caracas, Venezuela